The Cow's Bottom

By **Katie Dale**

Illustrated by
Cole Roberts

Chapter 1

Ever since he was very little, Jayden had loved acting. As a baby, he loved pretending to be a monster!

"GRRR!"

4/21   TEN

Books should be returned or renewed by the last
date above. Renew by phone **03000 41 31 31** or
online *www.kent.gov.uk/libs*

Libraries Registration & Archives

'The Cow's Bottom'
An original concept by Katie Dale
© Katie Dale

Illustrated by Cole Roberts

Published by MAVERICK ARTS PUBLISHING LTD

Studio 11, City Business Centre, 6 Brighton Road,

Horsham, West Sussex, RH13 5BB

© Maverick Arts Publishing Limited November 2020

+44 (0)1403 256941

A CIP catalogue record for this book is available at the British Library.

ISBN 978-1-84886-717-8

www.maverickbooks.co.uk

This book is rated as: Gold Band (Guided Reading)

Gold

As a toddler, he loved pretending to be a superhero!

"Whoosh!"

At primary school, he loved pretending to be a ghost!

"WOOO-OOO!"

Jayden couldn't wait to be in his first proper play.

"This year we are doing the play, *Jack and the Beanstalk*!" said his teacher, Miss Finch.

Jayden was determined to get a good role, so he practised all of them!

He auditioned for the role of Jack's mum. "Will you take the cow to market, Jack dearie?" he said sweetly.

He auditioned for the role of the Giant. **"Fee-fi-fo-fum!"** he bellowed.

But Jayden really wanted the main role of Jack.

"Ooh! Magic beans! Hurray!" he whooped, clicking his heels together.

Chapter 2

After the auditions, Jayden checked the
notice board nervously every day.
Then finally, Miss Finch put the cast list up!
Jayden rushed over excitedly.

Was he playing Jack's mum? No.

Was he playing the giant? No.

Was he... could he possibly be playing Jack?!

No.

Was he in the play at all? Yes.

Jayden stared at the list in horror.

He couldn't believe his eyes.

He was playing... **the cow's bottom!**

Jayden was shocked. Then he was sad.
Then he was cross. Then he went to see
Miss Finch.

"I don't want to be in the play!" he cried.

"What?" Miss Finch gasped. "But you're so
good at acting, Jayden!"

"Then why have you given me the role of the
cow's bottom?" Jayden asked. "I'm not even
the cow's head! Chen is! No one will see my
face!"

"I'm sorry I couldn't give you a bigger role this time, Jayden," Miss Finch said, patting his shoulder. "But we have to give the big roles to the older kids," she explained. "When you're older you'll get a bigger part."

"Oh," Jayden said sadly. "I see."

"But," Miss Finch smiled, "you are so good at acting that I want you to be Jack's understudy."

"What's an understudy?" Jayden frowned. "I thought Sol was playing Jack."

"Yes he is, but if Sol gets ill we'll need a great actor to step in and play Jack instead," Miss Finch said. "The show must go on! That's why I can't give you another big part - just in case we need you to play Jack on the night."

"Oh," said Jayden, feeling a bit better. "Okay. Great!" Maybe he would get to play Jack after all!

"Besides, the cow is one of the funniest parts in the whole play," Miss Finch said, smiling. "I know you will perform it well."

Jayden grinned. "I will."

Chapter 3

Rehearsals went really well, and everyone in the cast soon became good friends.

Jayden was really glad he hadn't quit the play. And it was actually great fun being the cow's bottom!

Chen and Jayden had a great time making up funny cow actions together. Jayden loved making everyone laugh!

But he made sure he knew Jack's lines well too – just in case.

Finally, the big night arrived!

Everyone gathered backstage to put their costumes on.

"Good luck," they whispered excitedly to each other.

Jayden smiled. He couldn't wait to go onstage!

"Everybody ready?" Miss Finch said. "It's show time!"

Chapter 4

Sol, Chen and Jayden stood in the wings, waiting for their cue.

"Oh Jack!" the girl playing Jack's mum cried. "Come here, dearie!"

"This is it!" Sol gulped, leading Jayden and Chen onstage.

Jayden's skin tingled with excitement as he felt the heat from the stage lights even through his costume.

"Will you take the cow to market, Jack dearie?" the girl playing Jack's mum asked.

"Mooooo!" Chen cried, as Jayden did a funny dance. The audience laughed and Jayden grinned. It was fun being in the play, whatever role he had.

But then something terrible happened. Sol forgot his words!

"Will you take the cow to market, Jack dearie?" the girl playing Jack's mum asked again.

Jayden nudged Sol, but Sol still didn't say anything.

Jayden gasped. Sol must have stage fright! Jayden's heart raced. If Sol couldn't play Jack, then Jayden would get the main role after all! Hurray! He was glad he'd learned all of Jack's lines just in case! The show must go on!

But then Jayden imagined how he would feel if he was standing there, frozen on the stage in front of everyone.

He would feel so embarrassed. So scared. So trapped. It would be terrible. Poor Sol.

Jayden knew all of Jack's lines, so he *could* help Sol. But if he did, Jayden would never get to play Jack...

"Will you take the cow to market, Jack dearie?" the girl playing Jack's mum asked a third time, her voice wobbling.
Jayden bit his lip. What should he do?

Chapter 5

Jayden took a deep breath and leaned towards Sol's ear. "No, I could never sell my Daisy," he whispered.

"No! I could never sell my Daisy!" Sol cried, relieved.

"She is the dearest thing in the world to me!" Jayden hissed.

"She really is the dearest thing in the whole wide world to me!" Sol cried, hugging Daisy. Jayden grinned - that hug wasn't in the script!

The rest of the show went really well. Jayden helped Sol with a few more lines, but luckily no one else noticed anything was wrong.

The audience laughed in all the right places.

And boo-ed in all the right places.

Then at the end they clapped loudly, and Daisy even got her own special cheer!

After the show, all the performers hurried backstage, buzzing with excitement and happiness.

As Jayden climbed out of his cow costume, Sol ran over and hugged him.

"Thank you *so* much for helping me with my lines, Jayden!" he cried. "I don't know what I'd have done without you! I was so nervous!"

"You're welcome," Jayden smiled. "We're a team, after all. The show must go on!"

Sol grinned. "You're a great actor, Jayden. And a really good friend. Thank you."

Jayden beamed.

"Congratulations, everyone!" Miss Finch cried, walking in with a huge smile. "You all worked so well together. The show was a huge success!"

Everyone cheered.

The End

Book Bands for Guided Reading

The Institute of Education book banding system is a scale of colours that reflects the various levels of reading difficulty. The bands are assigned by taking into account the content, the language style, the layout and phonics. Word, phrase and sentence level work is also taken into consideration.

Maverick Early Readers are a bright, attractive range of books covering the pink to white bands. All of these books have been book banded for guided reading to the industry standard and edited by a leading educational consultant.

Pink

Red

Yellow

Blue

Green

Orange

Turquoise

Purple

Gold

White

To view the whole Maverick Readers scheme, visit our website at

www.maverickearlyreaders.com

Or scan the QR code above to view our scheme instantly!